Greater Tibet

Where **earth touches** the **heavens**

Jimmy Lam

Ju K Tan

Times Editions
Marshall Cavendish

All photos by Jimmy Lam except
pages 88 (top), 90 (top), 100, 128 (top) by Ng Poh Ling
All words by Ju K Tan unless otherwise stated
Designed by Geoslyn Lim
Edited by Daphne Rodrigues

Jimmy Lam dedicates this book to his wife, Poh Ling.

Thanks to:
Theng Hwee, Siew Yim, Christine Gong at Country Holidays Travel, Singapore
Dakpa Kelden and Tenzin Lobsang
Zhang Fa Jun (Chengdu, Sichuan)

Published by **Times Editions** – Marshall Cavendish
An imprint of Marshall Cavendish International (Asia) Private Limited
A member of Times Publishing Limited
Times Centre, 1 New Industrial Road, Singapore 536196
Tel: (65) 6213 9288   Fax: (65) 6285 4871
Email: te@sg.marshallcavendish.com
Online Bookstore: www.marshallcavendish.com/genref

Malaysian Office:
Federal Publications Sdn Berhad (General & Reference Publishing) (3024-D)
Times Subang, Lot 46, Persiaran Teknologi Subang
Subang Hi-Tech Industrial Park, Batu Tiga, 40000 Shah Alam
Selangor Darul Ehsan, Malaysia
Tel: (603) 5635 2191   Fax: (603) 5635 2706
Email: cchong@tpg.com.my

National Library Board (Singapore) Cataloguing in Publication Data
Lam, Jimmy, 1963-
Greater Tibet : where earth touches the heavens / Jimmy Lam, Ju K. Tan. – Singapore : Times Editions, c2005.
p. cm.
ISBN : 981-232-747-9
1. Tibet (China) – Pictorial works. 2. Tibet (China) – Social life and
customs – Pictorial works. I. Tan, Ju Kuang, 1961- II. Title.
DS786
951.5 — dc21   SLS2004051233

Printed in Singapore by Utopia Press Pte Ltd

CONTENTS

A pilgrim turns the prayer wheels at the Labrang Monastery in Xiahe, Gansu Province. This influential monastery is one of the six most significant monasteries of the Gelug Buddhist order in Tibet. It occupies an enormous area and attracts scores of pilgrims throughout the Amdo region in eastern Greater Tibet.

FOREWORD

Geographers, travellers and explorers have always been fascinated by spectacular landscapes and exotic cultures that are remote and inaccessible. Few places are more remote and inaccessible than Greater Tibet, that part of Central Asia that is the homeland of the Tibetans and their extraordinarily durable, deep-rooted culture. It is a vast area that includes the Tibetan Autonomous Region and Lhasa, and the neighbouring areas of western Sichuan, Qinghai, Gansu and northwestern Yunnan. It embraces some of the most spectacular landscapes on earth, from the greatest Himalayan peaks to the arid wastes of the north.

Until recently, very few travellers from outside the area have been able to follow in the footsteps of the early explorers, like Sven Hedin, and those pursuing "the great race". Beyond the major cities, such as Lhasa and Chengdu, travel usually meant the rigours and challenges of expeditions. But that is changing. As roads are being improved and the air network extended, more and more travellers can explore and experience the extraordinary Tibetan world. Only two years ago, it took more than two days to travel from Chengdu to Kangding in western Sichuan. Today, it takes just five hours.

Jimmy Lam has been in the vanguard of the new wave of travellers. He has made 15 visits over a three-year period and put together a unique record, including many outstanding photographs, which provides a splendidly revealing insight into one of the world's great cultures and the breathtaking environment in which it is set. It is a record we can all enjoy in the comfort of home, and it is a record that provides an exciting preface for those of us seeking new frontiers to visit. This book is also a timely benchmark against which we can judge the changes that are just beginning to transform the area, for better or for worse.

Sir Ron Cooke
Past President of the Royal Geographical Society

the PHOTOGRAPHER and the AUTHOR

Jimmy Lam began his photographic pursuits in North America and Europe, inspired by the nature and wildlife there. Years after, he turned to Asia, travelling the region to preserve its peoples and cultures in still images. Tibet is his favourite subject. Lam is an associate of the Royal Photographic Society, and his photographs have appeared in several international magazines.

Ju K Tan left a banking career to toil as a freelance writer. Copywriting for nearly 10 years, he has spent the last three conceptualising and writing scripts for television. He has written six television series and two books, including *An Assembly of Tastes: The Culinary World of the United Nations*. Tan is also the editor of a monthly sports magazine, *Golf Asia*.

A rare moment in time, as the first rays of dawn shine like a spotlight on a *cham* dancer, leaving the rest of the group in the fading early-morning darkness. *Cham* dances are religious mask dances performed by Tibetan monks at monasteries during religious festivals.

JOURNEY INTO AN
ENCHANTED LAND

Of all the mystical destinations in the world, Tibet is perhaps the most arresting and intriguing. The vast, rugged terrain and extreme weather have invoked a plethora of legends and beliefs that form the foundation of life for an entire population. To anyone who has visited this beautiful land, Tibet is indeed a reflection, if not the personification, of the Shangri-La.

Jimmy Lam, for one, has been captivated by its spell.

In the last three years, Jimmy has been to Tibet 15 times. Unlike most, who base their journeys in Lhasa, Tibet's spiritual and economic capital, Jimmy has spread his time in Tibet across the far reaches of the land. To him, there is so much more to Tibet than the well-trodden path. Through his photographs, he has tried to encap-sulate the immensity and variety of the land in all its glory.

Finding refuge in monasteries and small guesthouses, and led by a few multi-lingual guides (who have become friends in the process), Jimmy has reached places not commonly associated with Tibet. From the Tibetan Autonomous Region that includes Nagqu, Shigatse and Tsetang, to Kangding and Litang in Sichuan, to Zhongdian in Yunnan and to the high plateaus of Qinghai, Jimmy has tried to cap-ture the diversity of the Tibetan world through the people's lifestyle, celebrations and religious devotion. Along the way, his eye for the land's natural disposition has produced a series of unbelievably vivid and poignant displays of colour and contrast that is unique to this part of the globe.

Jimmy has made his way through the Indian subcontinent, much of China and Indochina, and parts of Southeast Asia, documenting traditional landscapes and cultures that are threatened by globalisation and modernisation. Tibet has become his preoccupation.

"Tibet has one of the most fascinating cultures existing today. Tibetans have been able to preserve their customs and practices in the original form partly because of the inaccessibility of their land in the past. With improved travel infrastructure, Tibetans are becoming more exposed to the outside world. It remains to be seen how enduring their culture can be.

"The other reason why I have been so interested in documenting Tibetan culture is that many travel books focus on the area called the Tibetan Autonomous Region. I have seen much more of Tibet than that. Tibetan land and culture go beyond what most people think. I hope with this book to preserve the wider Tibetan area that includes parts of Qinghai, Yunnan, Gansu and Sichuan through my camera lens."

This book does not seek to be a compendium of facts, nor is it possible for it to cover every aspect of present-day Tibet. The mark of a photographer is his eye for detail, and in that respect Jimmy has parlayed his prowess in financial nitty gritty (honed by his experience as a securities analyst) into his passion for photography. His images of the land and people and their faith and festivals portray a Tibet we often only read about.

It has been said that Tibetans do not separate their traditions, religion and way of life, not to mention the fact that their beloved land has a bearing on all three. In the same way, it is hard to separate the photographer's conviction and emotion for his subject, from his pictures. Tibet has retained much of its character through centuries, and this book hopes to help in a small way the continued preservation of the beauty and meaning of this enchanted land and its blessed people.

Left: Tibetan women dressed up for a festival. Their hair is parted in the middle and decorated, often as a sign of love and respect for their husbands.

Siguniangshan (Four Maidens Mountain) shows its ragged peaks against the soft sky. The mountain is part of a scenic 450-square km area of Xiaojin County, Aba Prefecture, some 220 km from Chengdu, the capital city of Sichuan Province. The main peak towers 6,250 m over the surrounding terrain.

CHILDREN OF THE LAND

There is much to be said about a people being an integral part of the land on which they live. That postulation is more pertinent in Tibet than anywhere else. Certainly, a brief consideration of this breathtaking corner of the world conjures images of extremes and a magic that instills a strong, singular spirituality.

Tibetans call their home Khawachen, the land of snowy mountains. But that is a gross understatement of the land's dramatic, unrelenting geography. Tibet is enveloped by the highest peaks on earth, and its weather—capable of wide temperature differentials within a single day—can be tormenting and, at times, life-threatening.

One look at the general topography of Tibet gives the impression that something devastating must have occurred during the infancy of our planet and, in the process, given rise to the immeasurable beauty of this land. Not 100 million years ago, the Tethys Sea covered Tibet. That would explain how fossils of prehistoric sea creatures have been discovered here—4,000 m above sea level. The high plateaus and skyscraping mountains that define the Tibetan landscape formed about 45 million years ago, when

the Indian subcontinent collided with the Eurasian landmass and pushed it upwards. The mountains surrounding Tibet are still growing. Every year, their peaks rise about 10 cm closer to the heavens.

Geographically, Tibet is one of the world's natural wonders. The combination of latitude and altitude here produces a unique weather pattern bordering on the miraculous. If the land lay 15 degrees further north, it would be permanently under a layer of ice. And if it were located just a little south, it would experience desert temperatures like those in Egypt.

Tibet is bordered by three of the earth's greatest mountain ranges: Kunlun to the north, Karakoram to the west and the Himalayas to the south. Four of the world's tallest mountains guard Tibet's border with Nepal and Bhutan in the south, and where the Tibetan Plateau meets Qinghai Province lies one of the most remote and unexplored parts of the world outside the polar caps. Tibet's land elevation averages 4,000 m, with large areas rising above 5,000 m.

Left: Varying hues accentuate geographical differences in Kangding, Sichuan Province. Here, Tibetan tradition blends with the Chinese world to create an interesting economic and cultural exchange. Kangding is also an important stepping ground to Lhasa from Sichuan Province, and was historically the capital of the Tibetan kingdom of Chakla.

Right: The nomadic life is one of seasonal renewal. Setting up tent in the shadow of the highlands, Tibetan nomads try not to conquer but to live in harmony with the elements. They worship the wind, sky, water, rocks and mountains, embracing all that surrounds them.

From the ever-present snowcaps of the Tibetan highlands flow some of the planet's greatest rivers, such as the Indus, Ganges, Mekong, Irrawaddy, Yarlung Tsangpo and Yangtze. If we consider that nearly half the world's population receive water from these rivers, we can justly say that Tibet is not only the roof of the world but the fulcrum of much of its life as well.

The prevalent perception is that Tibet is a barren, largely uninhabited land of cold mountains and frozen tundra. The truth is that the Tibetan landscape has as much variety as any temperate country at the same latitude. Tibet's ecosystems range from semi-tropical to alpine. In the south, pines, firs and spruces fringe the border with Nepal. In the east, conifers and deciduous trees such as oak, birch and elm thrive on the more abundant rainfall. This subtropical area is also coloured by a rainbow of wildflowers.

Such ecological variety establishes the land as domain to some of the most endangered animals, including some that survive only in this very private corner of the planet and nowhere else. The white-lipped deer, black-necked crane, ibex, Tibetan antelope, blue sheep and snow leopard are on a list of 80 or so species that are in serious danger of extinction. There are also more than 30 endemic birds in Tibet, and nearly 500 bird species have been sighted in Tibet, predominantly around lakes and on plateaus.

Yet more common are marmots, weasels, gazelles and hares, and the indigenous, rather ubiquitous, yak. The musk deer lives in the Himalayan jungles along the southern border, and Tibet is the world's largest producer of musk. Tibet is also one of the last

refuges for the giant panda. Pandas in Tibet subsist on the indigenous bamboo of the southern areas.

The changing political landscape in Tibet makes defining its territory a little confusing. Tibet is largely known as the Tibetan Autonomous Region (TAR), an expanse of more than a million square km. Tibet as presented in this book consists of three distinct historical cultural regions: Ngari in the west, Utsang in the centre and Kham and Amdo in the east. Much of the eastern region—characterised by its high elevation, rugged mountains and barely explored terrain—has been seceded to the Chinese provinces of Qinghai and Sichuan.

With a relatively agreeable climate and the presence of the Yarlung Tsangpo River, the Utsang region is Tibet's agri-cultural, commercial and political heart. Its largest cities are Lhasa, Shigatse, Tsetang, Gyantse and Chamdo. In the north of Utsang is the Tibetan Plateau, the highest of its kind in the world, where dead lakes remain as rem-nants of the prehistoric Tethys Sea.

Left: The day's first rays of light cast an eerie glow on the Qionglai Mountains of Sichuan Province.

Right (top): With sunlight gone and frigid cold setting in, Tibet takes on a different mood. Temperatures plum-met and winds blow with a vengeance, transforming the mountainsides into areas of monochromatic treachery.

Right (bottom): Clouds often shroud the 6,740-m-high summit of Meilixueshan in Diqing Prefecture, Yunnan Province. Pilgrims travel from all over Tibet to circum-ambulate this important religious mountain.

The land's elevation takes a dip as one travels east towards Kham, the eastern section of Tibet that has merged with the Yunnan and Sichuan provinces. Here, great rivers such as the Yangtze and Mekong have gouged gigantic valleys rivaling the grand canyons of North America.

From the unforgiving geology of Tibet, a people have emerged who not only meet its challenge but also embrace it as a blessing from God. Tibetans regard their environment not as an adversary but as something that simply is, and will be for all time. They try to understand and explain the realities of nature through myth and legend. Stories about the depths of the lakes or about the invisible winds that sweep through the plains help Tibetans make sense of life and find harmony in their existence.

Left: Instead of snowy peaks, the south of Qinghai Province is dominated by emerald slopes. This region, reaching altitudes of around 2,500 m, has a fitting name in Qinghai, which is Chinese for green sea.

Opposite (top): Evergreen trees mark the hilly, remote route to Diqing, Yunnan Province. The prefecture is home to three counties: Zhongdian, Deqin and Weixi. The region is a cultural crossroads, bridging the gap between the Tibetan world and the Chinese mainland in Sichuan Province. Tibetans live here among other ethnic groups, such as the Lisu, Naxi, Yi and Bai.

Opposite (bottom): An early winter morning brings a spiritual calm to the plains of Tsetang. Tibet's third largest city is situated in the Yarlung Tsangpo river valley. The Yarlung basin is believed to be the cradle of ancient Tibetan civilisation where kings maintained their courts long before Buddhism came.

Far left: The almost-black yak-hair tents of Tibetan nomads contrast with the colours of summer in Shiqu County, Sichuan Province.

Left: Grazing time for a yak herd. Yaks are the livestock and lifeline of Tibetans. Tibetans drink yak's milk, eat yak meat and make tents from yak hair and boots from yak hide. After sheep and goats, yaks are the next most common animals in Tibet.

Below: As the sun begins to set, another yak herd make their way home to a village in the foothills. Tibetans take great care of their yaks—their *nor*, or wealth. They look for new grazing areas during the year, leading the herd uphill in summer and down into the valleys in winter.

Left: Fast-flowing streams and rivers characterise the rugged road from Chengdu in Sichuan Province to Zhongdian in Yunnan Province.

Above: Between Kangding and Litang in Sichuan Province, a river courses through a mountainside painted with the accents of autumn.

Right: A waterfall at Jiuzhaigou, the valley of nine villages, in Jiuzhai County, Sichuan Province. The valley is the source of several rivers, such as the Jialing, which forms part of the Yangtze system.

Right: It is May and still winter in the higher parts of Qinghai Province. Nomads try to keep warm in the valleys. Their tents are made from thickly woven yak hair to keep out the cold.

Far right: Autumn's hues radiate the beauty of the road between Xiangcheng in Sichuan Province, and Zhongdian in Yunnan Province. Up here, at an altitude of 3,276 m, the weather never gets warm. At the height of summer in July, the temperature rarely rises beyond 14°C.

Far left: When spring and summer arrive, wildflowers bloom throughout the countryside, breaking the monotony of winter's gray. Much of the flora in Tibet is alpine. Rhododendrons, cypresses and junipers predominate at altitudes above 3,000 m.

Left (top and bottom): The woodlands of western Sichuan Province are a hotbed of biodiversity. The alpine coniferous forests here are rich in spruces, firs and pines and are a source of geothermal energy.

Below: In October in western Sichuan Province, amid waterfalls and streams fresh from summer, leaves turn red, gold, and orange.

Wildflowers and fall foliage attract many visitors to Jiuzhaigou, Litang and Miyalou in Sichuan Province between June and October. Besides being a sight to behold, flora in Tibet have a spiritual significance. Juniper, for instance, is considered sacred, a popular abode for specific spirits. Juniper branches are often offered in sacrifices, and juniper berries used as a narcotic to induce trances in religious performances.

Opposite: A river in a narrow valley on the way to Aba Prefecture reflects the orange of nearby mountains. In some parts of Tibet, rivers freeze in winter and flow again in spring, when the mountain snows thaw.

Far left: Jiuzhaigou is famous for its alpine lakes, waterfalls and rivers. Known as a fairy land on earth for its primeval beauty, the valley of nine villages is a UNESCO World Heritage Site.

Left (top and bottom): Winter brings a different beauty to the Tibetan landscape. Natural ice sculptures and water sprays splash the landscape with shades of blue.

Preceding spread: Alpine summer wildflowers bloom in the provinces of Qinghai and Sichuan between June and August.

Left & Below: Prayer flags flap in the winds that sweep through the great plains of Tibet. Tibetans believe the winds brought forth life on earth.

Left: Prayer flags arranged in a tent-like structure overlook a village in Aba Prefecture, Sichuan Province.

Below: Tibetans design and build their homes based on practicality and belief rather than aesthetics. From solitary tents to villages, Tibetan shelters are simple structures adapted to the natural environment, enabling their inhabitants to live off the land in a quiet, non-intrusive way.

Right: A cute, rosy-cheeked child in Aba Prefecture. Tibetans are believed to have descended from nomadic Mongol tribes migrating from the Asian Steppes more than two millennia ago to the Yarlung Tsangpo river valley in what is now the Tibetan Autonomous Region.

Opposite: The elaborate clothes Tibetans sometimes wear contrast to the starkness of the landscape. At a prayer ceremony in Litang in autumn, devotees bring out their colourful best, which may include animal skins and ivory jewellery.

FOLLOWERS OF DESTINY

If a land shapes a people, it is little surprise that Tibetans are the way they are. The natural landscape all around them is at once breathtaking and fear-inspiring.

Mountains that touch the clouds fence Tibetans in and the rest of the world out. Temperatures that test the limits of human endurance persist year in and year out. The Tibetan's ability to survive in such an environment is a tribute to the power of the gods.

Tibetans believe that their existence began with heavenly beings. Legend tells how a Bodhisattva, Avalokiteshvara, sent his reincarnation in the form of a celibate monkey to meditate in a mountain in Tibet. There, he was approached by an ogress, who wanted to marry him. The monkey sought the advice of Avalokiteshvara and married the ogress. Their consummation produced six kinds of offspring: gods, demigods, hungry ghosts, denizens of hell, animals and people, from whom the Tibetans originated.

Scientific investigation traces the Tibetan people to Mongol nomads who ventured west and south from the Asian Steppes, seeking new pastures for their herds or new hunting grounds, some 2,500 to 3,000 years ago.

The descendants of the ancient Mongol nomads still live a life not too different from that of their ancestors. The Dokpa take refuge in tents and take their herds of yak, sheep or cattle out to pasture. They trade with farmers or city dwellers, exchanging their meat and dairy products for other produce and goods. The concept of trade is understandably very well-received among Tibetans. An old saying goes: "If religion is the heart of a Tibetan, then trade is his lungs." Certainly, for a country so devoid of natural resources, the ability and willingness to exchange what one has for something another has is not only sensible but also necessary.

Some Tibetan nomads lead a more intermediate lifestyle. They live as farmers most of the year and as nomads in summer. Like the Dokpa, they are free from the travails of modernism, living and working where they like, the forces of nature being the only influence on their travel plans.

True to their migratory nature, Tibetans may be found beyond their usual territory. They have wandered east across the Minjiang River onto the plains of Chengdu in the heart of Sichuan, crossed the Himalayan barrier and been absorbed into the population in Bhutan, Nepal and the Indian state of Sikkim, ventured west into the hill districts of Ladakh and Garhwal, and travelled to the valleys east of the Karakoram range, closer to the origins of Buddhism, which they regard with the utmost reverence.

The Tibetan way of life compared to the Western way of life is difficult to understand, if not difficult to believe. Polyandry—one woman having more than one husband at one time—is common. The dead are neither buried nor cremated. The Tibetan "sky burial" is one of the most exotic and macabre rituals in practice today. The deceased is carted to the top of a sacred hill to be dismembered and fed to vultures. The bones are ground up and either scattered, or molded into clay figurines to be kept by the family.

But to measure Tibetan thought against worldly wisdom is a fallacious exercise. Tibetans believe, as Buddhist doctrine instigates, that their lives on earth are temporary, part of a lengthy process of birth and rebirth before they reach nirvana. Therefore, their bodies after death are deemed meaningless, as their spirits continue to search for another entity—the subsequent renewed existence, hopefully, moving them closer to ultimate enlightenment. Understanding this important tenet of the Tibetan way of life explains much of their actions.

The spiritual tradition and physical surroundings of Tibetans bear an undeniable influence on them. To them, there is no delineation between what they do, what they believe and what eventually transpires. All aspects are intertwined; one action leads to another, and what occurs is a consequence of what happened before. It is inconceivable that their livelihood can be separated from their religious belief or from how they bring up their children. It is all one and the same, driven by a common aspiration derived from what they believe will happen to them in this life and the next.

As far as commercialism and technology have led the modern world, much can be said, and has been said, about the Tibetan way of life. Tomes have been written on how their approach is applicable to anyone and everyone. Truly, if we consider that the ready smiles and gentle disposition of Tibetans reflect a peace of mind not common in most parts of the world, then it only goes to show that there is indeed something special in this unique people.

Left: The infectious smile of a young monk resting in the summer grassland in Ganzi Prefecture in Sichuan reflects the peace that Tibetans find in simplicity, an uncommon privilege in our harried world. Ganzi is home to the great Garze Monastery, where more than 500 monks devote their lives to the teachings of the Buddha.

Top: A child sleeps on a pilgrimage to Lhasa in winter. Tibetan children are taught to endure hardship as a way of life. A child only 2 to 3 months old is stripped, rubbed with butter and left out in the cold for hours. That begins a process to build up the child's endurance of the rigorous weather that he or she will face growing up.

Centre: A Tibetan child gets a little distracted while being fed a meal. Living simple lives, with little contact with the outside world, Tibetan children tend to be very inquisitive.

Bottom: A young Tibetan nomad poses for the camera with his pet kid. Tibetans readily invite guests into their tents, and children eagerly show visitors their toys and pets. Pets are let into the house, but they often wind up as dinner when they "come of age".

Top: The elderly enjoy the respect of the young in Tibet. They are seen as the most important people in the household and are usually given prominent positions in the dining and guest rooms.

Right: A Tibetan woman accessorises from head to toe for a monastery ceremony in Litang. Her ornaments are not merely decoration for the occasion; they are symbols showing where she comes from.

Far right: A young girl collects cow dung with her bare hands to use as fuel. Tibetans use what they can in their resource-poor land.

The Tibetan home is organised around the extended family, with three generations living under one roof. Children and grandparents tend to spend a lot of time together.

Left (bottom): The nomad's diet is simple. The staple food is *tsampa*. Barley is roasted and ground into flour using a stone hand mill, then stirred into water or tea, or mixed with butter. The result, though bland, is filling and nourishing.

Right & Opposite (centre): Tibetan children are named (by their parents or by a high lama) not at birth but after the first month of life. There is no distinction between male and female names, and birthdays are often not celebrated.

Top: Horses are an integral part of Tibetan life, and children learn to ride from a very early age.

Bottom: A woman from Diqin packs a load of branches.

Left: A nomad tends his yak herd as the animals graze in the highlands between the counties of Chamdo and Suoxian in May, when the snow begins to melt. Yaks are an integral part of Tibetan life, and nomads often own a herd. The yak's ability to subsist in high country makes it an easy animal to move around.

Below: The sun sets on a herd of sheep in Maqin County in Guoluo Prefecture, Qinghai. Sheep are another kind of livestock raised by many Tibetans.

Bottom: Tibetan farmers use yaks to plough their fields. About five-sixths of the Tibetan population rely on the soil for subsistence. They grow potatoes, barley, buckwheat, turnips, peas, wheat and millet in the valleys.

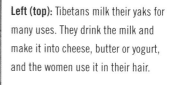

Left (top): Tibetans milk their yaks for many uses. They drink the milk and make it into cheese, butter or yogurt, and the women use it in their hair.

Centre: Yaks being herded in Qinghai. Yaks used as pack animals are never slaughtered. They are cared for by their owners as long as they live.

Far left (top): A homebound yak train bears goods their owners bought at their town of departure.

Far left (bottom): A group of Tibetan villagers encircle a runaway yak to try to recapture it.

Left (bottom): A cattle train in Qinghai. Many Tibetans rear cattle for meat. Herders do not slaughter their animals themselves. They consider it bad karma and often pay other people to do the job.

Top: People in Shigatse in the TAR collect soil from a river bed to use on their farms. Imagination is the key to survival in a land where resources are scarce. The centre of the Utsang region and the second largest city in the TAR, Shigatse has a population of about 450,000.

Bottom: It is early morning in Aba, and vendors are already out on the streets, hawking dried yak dung, which shops and restaurants buy to use as fuel.

Top: Nomads and semi-nomads depend on the soil for a different reason from farmers. Here in an area between Chamdo and Nagqu in the TAR, they are digging for worms to sell. The worms have medicinal uses.

Bottom: Tibetans plant a field of gold. The yellow-flowered oilseed rape plant is used to produce cooking oil.

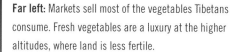

Far left: Markets sell most of the vegetables Tibetans consume. Fresh vegetables are a luxury at the higher altitudes, where land is less fertile.

Left (top): Farmers harvest wheat in Zhongdian. Other crops cultivated in the area include barley, potatoes, peas, rape and broad beans.

Left (bottom) & Below: As spring brings more sunshine, far-mers spread out their wheat harvest on rooftops to dry before processing it for further use.

Left: Given the lack of resources, it is no surprise that trade, mostly barter, has been the bellows of the Tibetan economy for centuries. Farmers and craftsmen come to the village several times a week to exchange produce and other goods for the nomads' meat and dairy products.

Below: A vendor shows off her nicely cleaned yak bones for sale.

Right (bottom): An old man runs his cobbler service in the streets of the small town of Xiahe in Gansu Province. With minimal infrastructure, local commerce is conducted outdoors. Small streetside stalls proliferate, catching the eye and wallet of passers-by.

Right (top): For a lack of department stores, clothes are commonly sold along the street. Festival time is when business really picks up.

Top: Horses give Tibetans on a simple pilgrimage to Maqin some reprieve from the long walk. Pilgrimages can last for months, and pilgrims can walk for hours on end between rest stops. On more serious pilgrimages, people repeatedly prostrate themselves on the ground throughout the entire journey. Tibetans consider it an honour and a privilege to embark on one of these arduous campaigns at least once in their lives.

Bottom: A group of Tibetans ride their horses to a horse festival. They bring with them yaks to be sold or to carry goods that they will buy at the festival. If the yak is an economic icon in Tibet, the horse is a spiritual one. Horses are strongly featured on prayer flags, and the wind horse is believed to fly prayers to the heavens.

Opposite: How they look is as important as how they perform. Horses get a wash by the river before heading out to the races.

Left: But sometimes it is hard work trying to get a horse to take a bath.

Below: A group of monks in Ganzi enjoy some leisure time with their horses. During summer, Tibetans sometimes get together in small groups to ride or race on horseback.

Right: Riders prepare to parade before the start of the races in Litang. Behind them, white tents have been set up in the field for the festival.

Opposite (main): Getting properly attired for a major celebration is a lot of work. This little girl gets help from her parents to put on her accessories: bells and shells on her pigtails; earrings and finger rings with gems; amber and silver bracelets; and necklaces speckled with cat's eye and pearl. Relatives come from faraway and camp out for days to watch the events, socialise and trade.

Opposite (top and centre): Camping out in summer is an annual activity among most Tibetans. While enjoying the great outdoors in the more tolerable months of the year, they engage in traditional games like tug-of-war or picking up sweets using their mouths.

Opposite (bottom): Young monks while away the time while waiting for an opera to begin in Ganzi. Opera festivals are held only in certain places, the most famous one being in Lhasa at the Norbulingka, the summer palace of the Dalai Lama.

Left: Tibetans gather from all around to watch riders show off their skill at the horse races in Zhongdian.

Nothing is without symbolism in Tibetan culture. Prayer flags, or *tar-chok*, depict auspicious icons such as the mystical wind horse, or *lung-ta*, which carries people's prayers on its back. Tibetans hang prayer flags in thanksgiving, to pray for prosperity or posterity, and sometimes to mourn the loss of loved ones. The fluttering of the flags is seen as a sign that their prayers are being carried to the heavens.

LIVING THE FAITH

Perhaps no concept is as synonymous to Tibet as Buddhism. Mention one and the other often follows close behind, such is the indivisible nature of the two. But the reality is that strong beliefs in a higher state of being existed in Tibet many years before Buddhism made its way here from India.

The main religion of Tibet before the introduction of the Buddha's teachings was Bon. The major tenet of this ancient religion was the maintenance of the cosmic order, and the careful relationship between people and the gods. This was a belief fraught with ritualistic practices—human sacrifice not withstanding—and where shamans had a hold on the people through complex rites. So deeply engraved was the Bon tradition in the psyche of the people that even when Buddhism arrived in the fifth century it could not completely eradicate customary Bon beliefs.

Buddhism arrived in Tibet during the reign of King Songtsen Gampo, who built the important Jokhang and Rampoche temples, and the fort in Lhasa where the Potala Palace now stands. Through the influence of Gampo's two wives—the Chinese Wen Cheng and the Nepali Bhrikuti—Buddhism gained a foothold in Tibet.

Then in A.D. 755 Gampo's successor, Thrisong Detsen, invited the Indian sage Padmasambhava to spread the Buddha's teachings to the Tibetan people, and Buddhism began to take flight in Tibet.

But even though Tibetans embraced the scriptures introduced by Padmasambhava, they could not fully abandon their Bon beliefs, which had subsisted for so long. As a compromise, many Bon practices were incorporated into a hybrid version of Buddhism now commonly referred to as Tantric Buddhism, where the transcendental leanings of the origins of Buddhism were married to the mystical practice of the ancient Bon religion.

Over centuries, with Buddhism subsiding in China, Nepal and India, Tibetan Buddhism grew from strength to strength. By the ninth century, Tibet had become the most devout Buddhist territory in the world. Tibetans took in the faith and made it their own. It became an integral part of their lives, enhancing a religious homogeneity not seen anywhere else in the world. Such adherence to a spiritual belief exists to this day.

Left: Red, blue, green, yellow and white are the predominant colours of prayer flags all over Tibet. They represent the elements of nature: fire, sky, water, earth and clouds.

Right: Prayer-flag displays differ from region to region. In an area of Qinghai, flags are arranged in a conical formation rising towards the sky. Star formations may also be seen in the area.

Given Tibet's fragmented history and centuries of political and cultural change, Tibetan Buddhism took several segregating deviations. Different sects, or orders, evolved with varying beliefs and practices.

The disciples of Padmasambhava started the Nyingma order, also known as the Red Hat sect, in the 12th century. In the 13th century, the Sakya order arose, led by Kunga Gyaltsen. Two centuries later, Tsong Khapa, a native of Amdo, founded the Gelug order, also known as the Yellow Hat sect, which swept through the land and altered the entire religious fabric. Tsong Khapa became the first Dalai Lama of Tibet.

There may be differences among Tibet's Buddhist groups, but they are all united by unwavering devotion. So strong is the role of religion in Tibetan life that it pervades a person's time from birth to death. Not a day goes by without Tibetans attributing some aspect of their lives to their faith. The most devout might devote themselves to a monastery. Some make periodic pilgrimages to sacred places or temples. All are familiar with the tantric chants, such as the omniscient "*Om Mani Padme Om*", which resonates with an immaculate frequency and depth throughout Tibet's cultural landscape.

Studying the religious following in Tibet is a thorough exercise in iconographic implication. Tibetan Buddhism is identified and made potent by physical symbols of meta-physical significance. Prayer beads, *mani* stones (mantra-inscribed stones) and the *thangka* (religious painting),

tar-chok (prayer flag), *chorten* (stupa) and mandala (a circular meditational device) all reinforce the Tibetan's conviction that a higher state of being exists, and their quest to reach that spiritually elevated plane.

To outsiders, it might be hard to see where religion ends and mysticism begins in the Tibetan's world. This is where lamas inspire through their wise teachings and temples are deemed so sacred that people walk hundreds of miles to visit—and the more difficult the journey, the more significant the pilgrimage. Ultimately, Tibetans see the present life as transient, a mere stepping stone to another life. Tibetans understand where they came from and what they have to do in this life to attain a better one in the next realm on the inevitable road to true enlightenment.

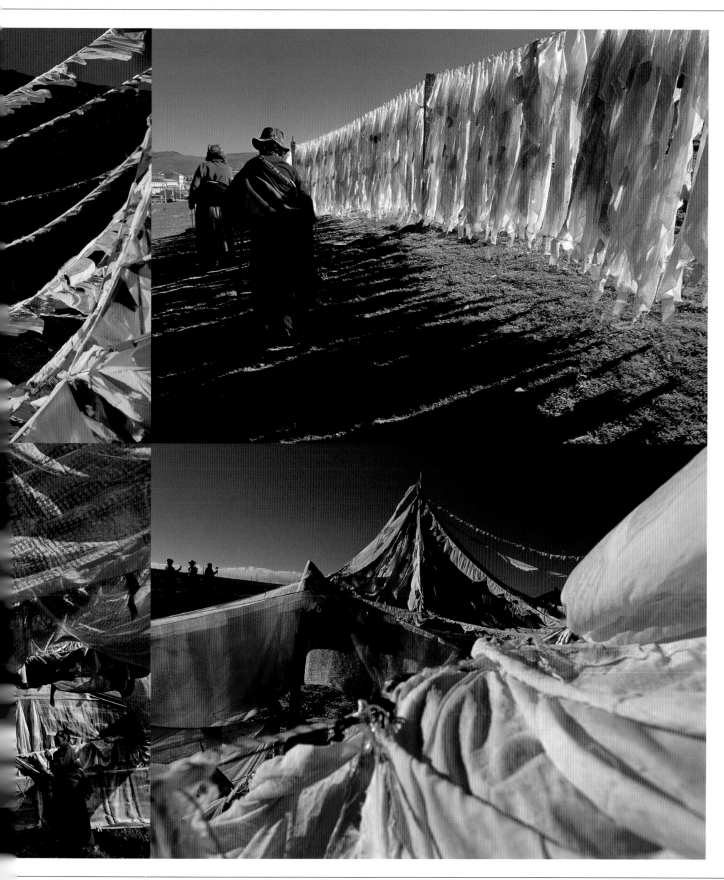

Top (left): On a hillside near Lhasa, prayer flags in the traditional five colours flutter in the wind, calling Tibetans to keep in mind the Buddha's teachings. The wind is seen as the expression and energy of the mind.

Top (right): Devotees circumambulate prayer flags in worship. The block-printed mantras on the flags wish all beings happiness, enlightenment, protection and freedom from suffering.

Bottom (left): Prayer flags are attached to chords and strung between poles or trees. The cotton or polyester flags are protected from neither sun nor rain. Their replacement represents a renewal and is an important part of their ritual significance.

Bottom (right): Prayer flags hang in line with the four points of the compass, conveying blessings to the four corners of the earth.

Top (left): The surface of a bell in the Jokhang Temple in the heart of Lhasa is ornately decorated with Buddhist imagery. More than a metre tall and almost a metre wide, the bell is one of many icons that draw pilgrims and tourists alike to the mystery-shrouded temple.

Top (right): The image of the mystical wind horse is sometimes rendered on thin square pieces of paper. Tibetans throw these pieces of paper to the wind so that the wind horse will carry their prayers sky-wards to the gods.

Bottom: Cloth or canvas paintings called *thangka* in the monastery at Litang feature colourful Buddhist icons as a source of religious inspiration. During major festivals, *thangka* measuring hundreds of square metres are displayed on mountainsides in Tibet.

Opposite: Inscribed with Buddhist scripture or imagery, *mani* stones are found around monasteries or in villages as symbols of worship and thanksgiving.

Left: The line between nature and religion is fine in Tibet, where many mountains and rivers are considered sacred. Stones piled by pilgrims and villagers mark this site near Tsetang as sacred.

Below: A house out in the country is enshrouded with a pagoda-like *tar-chok* structure.

Bottom: Yak horns prominently placed outside a village are believed to reinforce the power of *mani* stones to protect people from the torrent of nature or of evil forces. When Tibetans come across such religious piles in their journey, it is not uncommon for them to circumambulate the piles as a display of their religious piety.

Right (top): The Ganden Monastery stands in quiet solitude on a mountainside 40 km east of Lhasa. It was built by Tsong Khapa, the founder of the Gelug order, Tibet's most widespread Buddhist group. Tsong Khapa began building at the end of the 14th century and finished in the early 15th century. He named the monastery Ganden, Tibetan for Tushita, the pure land where the Buddha Maitreya resides. Tsong Khapa died in 1419, two years after the main hall of the monastery was consecrated.

Right (bottom): The Yumbu Lagang sentinels over the patchwork plains of the Yarlung Tsangpo river valley. According to some accounts, this is the oldest building in Tibet, its foundations laid 2,000 years ago. Its history is shrouded in legend. Some say it was built as the home of King Nyentri Tsenpo, who was purportedly sent down from the heavens. The Yumbu Lagang's structure hints at its use as a fort in the past, but it is now used as a place of worship.

Left (top): Mystical Zhongdian, known in Tibetan as Gyalthang, recently changed its name to Shangri-La. Whether this part of Yunnan actually is the forgotten oasis is arguable, but its beauty is undeniable. The Bita and Napa Lakes and Haba Snow Mountain nature reserves are part of the Three Parallel Rivers of Yunnan Protected Areas and are listed as a UNESCO World Heritage Site.

Left (bottom): Perched on Marpo Ri, or Red Mountain, about 130 m above Lhasa, the Potala Palace casts a magical shadow over its surroundings. This awe-inspiring monument is truly one of the wonders of Eastern architecture and, to the outside world, has become synonymous with Lhasa. This is where King Songtsen Gampo built his palace in the seventh century. Work on the Potala began with the nine-storey Karpo Potrang, or White Palace, in 1645 when the fifth Dalai Lama decided to use the location as the headquarters of his Gelug government. About 50 years later, the larger Marpo Potrang, or Red Palace, was added to complete the Potala.

Above: Stupas, or *chorten*, adorn the landscape in a village on the outskirts of Dege, the Kham region's cultural heartland. These pointed crowns may stand alone in an open space or sit atop a building. Originating in India, stupas are one of the many icons of Buddhism and represent the Buddha's wisdom. Originally built to house relics of the Buddha, they occasionally contain the cremated remains of high lamas.

Right: Morning breaks, and the air is filled with the scented smoke of burning incense in a Tibetan village. Incense burning is a centuries-old Buddhist practice. The arresting aromas help to soothe and calm the restless mind. Incense is typically made of jasmine flowers, rose petals, sandalwood, cedar bark and other natural ingredients that, when burnt, emit a musky scent that permeates the air and the senses.

Right (top): Worshippers make their way across the Yarlung Tsangpo River in a motorboat en route to the Samye Monastery not far from Lhasa. The Yarlung Tsangpo river valley is considered the birthplace of Tibetan civilisation and is also one of the most fertile areas of Tibet. The Samye Monastery has the distinction of being Tibet's first monastery.

Right (bottom): Helpers carry supplies for pilgrims. Making a pilgrimage to a holy place is considered an honour and a once-in-a-lifetime obligation by Tibetan Buddhists. The journey covers many miles and takes many days, sometimes months. Pilgrims travel to Lhasa from as far as the Kham region.

Opposite: The conviction and devotion of Tibetan Buddhists are not to be trifled with. Pilgrims prostrate themselves after every few steps as they make their way on foot to their destination.

Left: In a mountain pass just outside Lhasa, pilgrims take a break from their journey to rest in a rock enclosure built by pilgrims before them as a shelter from the strong winds of the high mountains. Tibetan Buddhists consider the pilgrimage a chance to remove themselves from the familiar and enrich the potential of their being.

Above: Pilgrims from the same village head towards Lhasa, each carrying a few belongings and a walking stick. A pilgrimage is both a shared and a personal experience. Despite its arduous nature, it builds bonds between companions and helps individuals refocus their lives and reflect on how they relate to what is sacred.

Far left: A fish-eye lens catches the view of a sea of prostrating pilgrims, passing villagers and curious tourists, from the roof of the Jokhang Temple in the middle of winter. This pilgrimage destination consists of not just the Jokhang Temple but also the Nangkhor corridor inside it and the Barkhor and Lingkhor areas around it.

Left (top and bottom): The forecourt to the Jokhang Temple has great commotion potential, but pilgrims and devotees are generally well-behaved, concentrating on their personal devotion to the sacred place. Prostrating may appear to outsiders as a form of asceticism, but Tibetan Buddhists do it with complete conviction.

Top (both): Pilgrims and devotees prostrate themselves in the doorway of the Jokhang Temple in the direction of the Jowo Sakyamuni statue inside. The statue was given to King Songtsen Gampo by his Chinese wife, Wen Cheng, as part of her dowry. The temple was originally called Trulnang, which means the temple of magical appearance. After the statue was moved here, the temple was renamed Jokhang, which means the shrine of the Jowo.

Bottom: Tibetan nuns take a break from their three-month pilgrimage from Ganzi to Lhasa. Tibetan women enjoy a somewhat higher social status than do women in certain other Asian cultures, but they are still regarded as inferior to men. Regardless of how stringently Buddhist nuns adhere to the restrictions of their religion, they can never be fully ordained as monks are in the *sangha,* the monastic community.

Opposite: A young Tibetan pilgrim ties new prayer flags to an existing structure of prayer flags in the Maqin area. The structure keeps growing as devotees keep adding flags.

Above: Spinning prayer wheels is as natural to Tibetans as breathing. They spin the wheels and recite mantras several times during the course of the day. These actions are woven into the fabric of Tibetan life.

Right: Hollow canisters strung up and braced by wooden structures make it easy for people to walk by for a spin. Tibetan prayer wheels in much larger sizes are more common in monasteries or pilgrimage sites. There are also miniature handheld versions of the prayer wheel that Tibetans can carry around.

Far right (top): Prayer wheels are typically inscribed with mantras inside. When someone spins the wheels, the mantras are believed to send blessings into the world.

At sacred places or pilgrimage sites, it is common to see these wheels arranged in a "prayer path". As pilgrims pass this line, they spin the wheels, thus releasing good tidings into the atmosphere.

Far right (bottom): A Tibetan holds up a picture of a deceased friend or relative while circumambulating a sacred site. Tibetan Buddhists believe in a cycle of death and rebirth until one achieves nirvana, or absolute enlightenment. There are many death-related rites and superstitions among Tibetans. For example, they are not allowed to express their grief in the home immediately after a death, as that may lure the consciousness of the deceased to be bound to its previous home and family.

Left (bottom): Tibetans circumambulate a monastery in Aba. Tibetans believe that circumambulation allows them to discover a sense of being centred and a clarity of being in the present.

Left (top): On a crystal-clear day in summer, Tibetans carry prayer flags in an outdoor procession near Maqin, Guoluo Prefecture, Qinghai. Located within the vicinity is Machen Kangri, a 6,282-m sacred mountain that symbolises the Amdo region.

Above: Villagers in Tongren in Qinghai parade with flags during the harvest, or summer, festival. The festival takes place in several villages each year, moving from one village to the next over a 10-day period. Tongren is a significant centre of Tibetan art, in particular *thangka* painting and appliquéing.

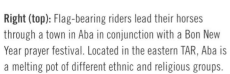

Right (top): Flag-bearing riders lead their horses through a town in Aba in conjunction with a Bon New Year prayer festival. Located in the eastern TAR, Aba is a melting pot of different ethnic and religious groups.

Right (bottom): Monks bring out a large *thangka* for display around the Kumbum Monastery near Xining, the capital of Qinghai. A *thangka* is often displayed on hillsides during important religious festivals.

Above: Monks of Tibet's oldest spiritual tradition, Bon, circumambulate monasteries often in a counterclockwise direction. Bon was purportedly founded by Tonpa Shenrab, who lived in a mythical land called Olma Lung Ring, linked by some scholars to Mount Kailash, a religiously significant mountain.

Opposite: A Tibetan monk ceremonially breaks a pole, following an ancient Bon practice. Bon and Buddhism have many similarities. It is said that the two share the same goals but have different paths. They also have in common certain concepts, such as rebirth and karma, and rituals. Bon iconography is embedded in ancestor worship, the invocation of spirits and the exorcism of demons.

Right: In thanksgiving for the harvest, the people of Tongren present food offerings to their deities in a temple. The offerings include cakes made of butter, yogurt, barley flour and honey. They represent the consecration of one's intentions to benefit others, and are a reminder of the importance of generosity.

Left: Monks unravel a *thangka* on a hillside at the Kumbum Monastery during the Saga Dawa festival. The monastery attracts many tourists, but Tibetans make up most of the Saga Dawa crowd. They come from distant villages to witness the unravelling of the *thangka* and to touch it.

Above: Full-fledged Bon monks one day they may be, but for now these children at a monastery in Aba rush off to play as soon as a New Year prayer ceremony ends.

Right: Lamas bless devotees at the end of a prayer ceremony at the Dzogchen Monastery, near the town of Dege in western Sichuan. The teachings at this major Nyingma monastery are well-known in the Western world. The monastery is an important pilgrimage destination not only for Tibetans but also for Buddhists from outside Tibet.

Right (top): Monks of the Nyingma order, the oldest school of Tibetan Buddhism, receive holy water at the Dzogchen Monastery after a five-day prayer event. The monks drink some of the water and pour the rest on their heads.

Right (bottom): Monks at a monastery in Chamdo debate Buddhist scripture. A leader stands in the centre of the group and challenges their knowledge. Discussion is an integral part of monastic training, as it helps the monks memorise the sacred texts. The monks' disciplinary code is derived from that of the early monastic community many centuries ago. Present-day practice may deviate from the original rules, and monks often debate the applicability of ancient rules in today's context.

Left (top): Concentration is key for these Tibetan monks as they meditate on the meaning of the chants at a prayer ceremony. Different monasteries have different styles of tantric chanting, some with amazing vocal dexterity. At the Gelug colleges of Gyuto and Gyume, for example, monks use their voices to chant chords, that is, different notes at the same time, creating an extraordinary sound.

Left (bottom): Many Tibetan families place their children in monasteries at a very early age. Entering the monastic life is a source of great pride, but it takes many years before the young monks -in-training reach the level of maturity needed to qualify for full ordination.

Left: A smile of innocence lights up the faces of young boys entrusted to the monasteries for a religious upbringing. In addition to the honour to be gained, there is an economic reason for sending boys into the religious life at such a tender age. Often, it boils down to a family being unable to bring up the child on their own.

Right (top): Monks blow the Tibetan long horn, or *rag dum*, to create a form of tantric resonance. This unique work of Tibetan art is usually made of copper or brass and measures about 2 to 2.5 m. It makes a sound akin to that of a trumpet, but in the hands of a skilled player, it can produce more than one note.

Far right (top): Tibet's monasteries may differ structurally, but inside they are all adorned with intricate icons reflecting the image of the Buddha and other deities that are significant in the institution's beliefs. Typically, each monastery has a hall where monks gather to meditate and chant or to celebrate an event.

Far right (bottom): Butter milk, a staple drink in Tibet, is served to monks during breaks in prayer ceremonies. Yak-butter tea is present everywhere. For something more potent, Tibetans drink *chang*, made from fermented barley.

Right (bottom): Pilgrims often honour icons at the Jokhang Temple, the House of Lords, with white scarves called *hada*. Devotees may present the scarves to the lamas, who wear them over their shoulders as a symbol of blessings, or leave the scarves amidst the statues.

Left: Scripture study is an integral part of monkhood. Monasteries are centres of learning. Some, such as the great Gelug monasteries of Drepung and Ganden, consist of colleges called *dratsang*. Monks are assigned to residences within each college depending on the region they come from.

Far left (top): After the long road to full ordination, not all monks become scholars or spiritual leaders. Many serve their monasteries in more mundane tasks, such as cooking and cleaning, besides keeping their regular prayer times.

Far left (corner): The glow of butter lamps in a Tibetan temple creates a mystical ambience. Butter lamps are found in almost any temple and are typically fueled with yak butter. The lamp light is symbolic of the wisdom of the awakened mind, free of all delusion and obfuscation.

Far left (bottom): A mandala about a metre in diameter is designed out of coloured sand at the monastery in Litang for a prayer ritual, after which the monks destroy the mandala, symbolising their detachment from material things. The mandala is one of the most arresting and intricate icons of Tibetan Buddhism. But its true meaning and premise are not etched in stone. It is a special "palace" in the imagination of the meditator. Each object or deity in the mandala represents an aspect of wisdom or a principle that the meditator needs to follow.

Left: A Tibetan monk enjoys a little solitude while painting a *thangka*. *Thangka* painting is an act of devotion, and the process is as important as the product.

Above: Monks begin the long road to ordination at varying ages, often as children. Not everyone makes it to the end, but for those who do, it is a great honour to achieve the full *gelong* vows.

Right: Meditation is an important part of monastic life. Tibetan Buddhism dictates that to be a healthy member of society, one must first put one's own life in order. Meditation helps one to be calm, controlled and self-aware. The Tibetan word for meditation, *gom*, means to familiarise oneself with an idea. In Buddhism, it means to familiarise oneself with a spiritual concept and make it part of one's consciousness.

Small pieces of paper rain down in clouds of incense smoke during the New Year festival. In this most auspicious time, Bon and Buddhist practices reach a peak in beckoning good fortune for the coming year.

CELEBRATING LIFE

The Tibetan's life is a complex blend of fate and deeds aimed at making the path to enlightenment smoother. Surrounded by treacherous mountain ranges and subsisting on a barren land at the mercy of tempestuous weather, Tibetans would appear to be caught on the verge of survival. Uncannily, life in Tibet is a series of celebrations.

From the first day of the lunar calendar to the last, the journey from one year to the next is marked by festivals that not only pay tribute to the gods and ancestors but also guide the road of the pilgrims on earth to nirvana.

Festivals in Tibet are not always religious, though. Tibetans are thankful for simple things, things that people in other parts of the world might take for granted. The coming of spring, the advent of the harvest, even the dawning of a clear blue sky when the weather turns agreeable—these are all worthy of getting out in one's best clothes to celebrate life with family, friends and the larger community. When summer comes, all Tibetans seem to pack their bags and head for the great outdoors. Pitching tents, they sing, dance and play under the endearing watch of the enduring sun during these longest of days.

The secular festivals celebrate the Tibetan's life through the course of the year. They are about the fruits of the people's labour and the continued success of their trials and tribulations. Tibetans go to the fields and sing songs that grew out of their livelihood, their dances mimicking the motions of the farm harvesters. These joyous activities egg on the growth of the soil and the renewal of the land, strengthening the close-knit community.

Horses are highly venerated among the Tibetan people, and many of their secular festivals feature these gallant beasts. The ancient king Trisong Detsen was reportedly killed while watching a horse race in Lhasa, and pre-Buddhism shamans associated horses with transcendence. In a land where roads hardly existed and motor vehicles were a mere figment of imagination, horses were the swiftest way to travel. The grandeur of the horse evoked legends like Gesar of Ling, the epic king with supernatural powers who ruled the land astride his winged horse. Over centuries, Tibet's horses became legendary across Central Asia, and their warrior riders were regarded with fear and admiration.

In more contemporary times, horse events have been much looked forward to during the Tibetan year. Racing, trick riding, or parading in festive ostentation, horse and rider participate in various events that underscore the reliance and inseparability of the two.

Although secular occasions are myriad in Tibet, religious festivals maintain their revered significance. Of the most important are the activities that herald the coming of the new year. As the lunar calendar begins another cycle, Tibetans—religious or otherwise—across the land gather to embark on activities that beckon prosperity and success. These activities make up the Losar festival and typically last from the first to the third day of the new year. On occasion, tens of thousands of monks descend on Lhasa for the new-year prayer, and Tibetans adorn their homes with strips of red and white cloth. Canopies and *thangka* paintings are renewed across the land, making this the most colourful time of the year.

As the new moon rises, usually around February or March, debts need to be settled and houses cleaned during this greatest of great times. Tibetans pay tribute to the ancestors, monks perform ancient ceremonies to drive out negative forces and everyone engages in rites to dispel obstacles and ensure a harmonious transition to the new year.

As the year progresses and the seasons change, many festivals celebrate landmark events in the history of Buddhism in Tibet. The Monlam festival carries on where the New Year celebrations end in the first month of the year. Then, in the fourth Tibetan month, the Saga Dawa festival reminds of the day the Buddha, or Sakyamuni, attained nirvana. In the fifth month, the Buddha Unfolding festival is a sight to behold. Celebrated in the Tashilhunpo Monastery, the festival features gigantic

Left: A devotee kicks off the New Year during the Great Prayer festival by throwing *tsampa*, or ground barley, into the air and shouting "*Lha Gya Lo*", which means "May the gods be victorious". Tibetans follow the lunar calendar but remove inauspicious days, so that there may be, for example, two third days in a particular month and no sixth day.

Far left: Despite the cold winter weather, Tibetan families gather for a picnic to welcome the fortune that awaits them in the new year.

Left: Monks gather to begin a ceremony on the last day of the year in Litang. The Losar festival often sees Tibetans pulling out all the stops in closing the year, with elaborate activities such as prayer ceremonies and mask dances.

thangka paintings depicting the Buddha and other deities on the walls of the monastery. The festival has survived for half a century, and each year thousands of pilgrims and monks pay tribute to the Buddha through outward displays of devotion during this time.

While modernisation and globalisation are inevitable in the future of Tibet, the people's adherence to tradition and custom gives rise to a deeply uniting force. Their celebrations are all-powerful, the hold of religion and a desire for a better life integral to their aspirations and sense of being. Their festivals are but a way for them to hold on to their revered past, and a manifestation of their devotion to the way things were and will be.

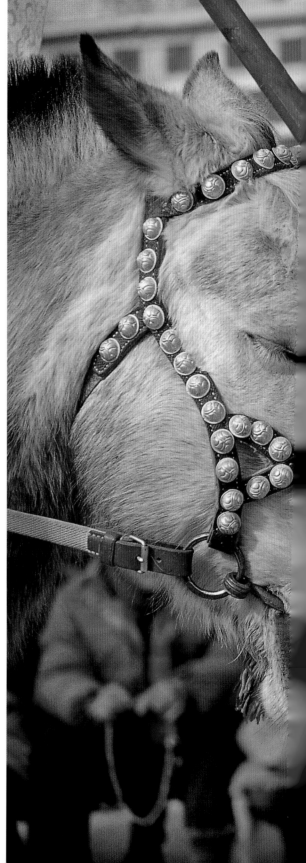

Above: During Monlam, monks from all the Tibetan Buddhist sects typically ascend the Jokhang to pray to Sakyamuni's image. While the monks pray, the whole of Tibet celebrates with religious dances and parades. This grandest of festivals can stretch for weeks as elaborate religious ceremonies coincide and share significance with military pageants, archery contests and horse races.

Right: A Tibetan parades in full regalia for the Monlam festival in Aba, where riders carry coloured flags and walk with their horses to the monastery. Started in A.D. 1409 by Tsong Khapa, Monlam falls on the fourth day of the first lunar month and is probably the most important religious festival in the Tibetan calendar.

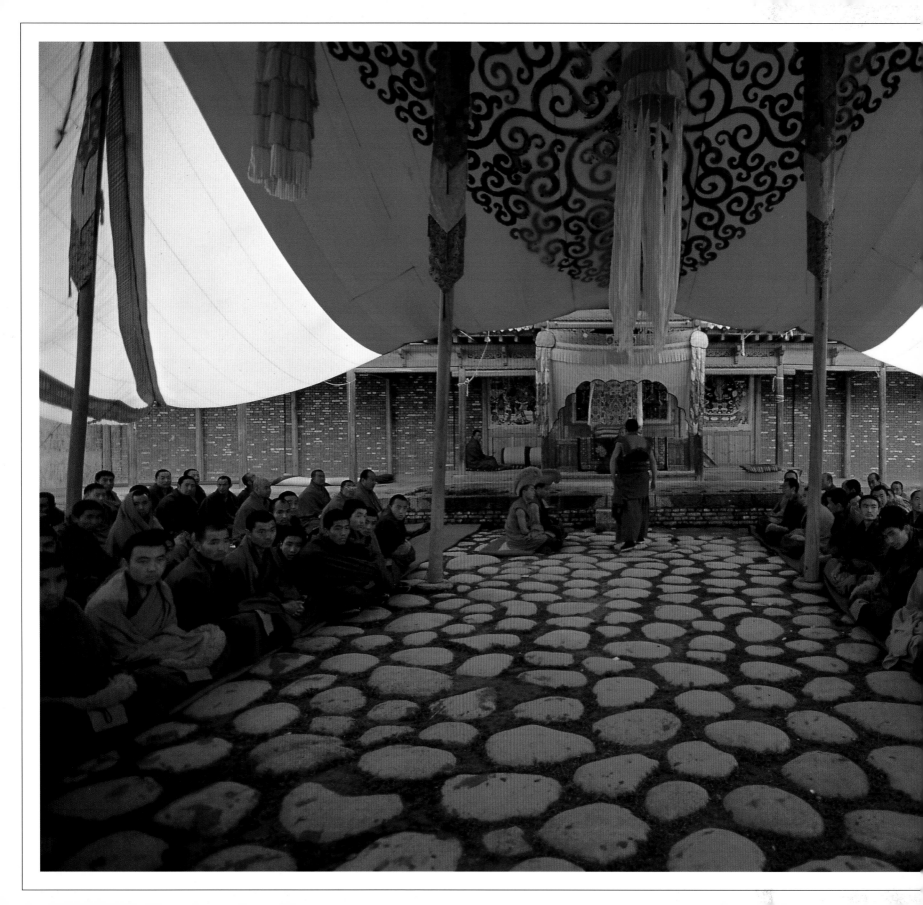

Left (top and bottom): Monks resonate in prayer during Saga Dawa, one of the more significant occasions on the Tibetan festival roster. Saga Dawa falls on the 15th day of the fourth lunar month and commemorates the Buddha's birth and attainment of nirvana.

Far left: Under a crimson shade, Tibetans await a ceremony during the Saga Dawa festival. Pilgrims gather in major religious centres throughout Tibet during Saga Dawa. They refrain from killing animals or eating meat, believing that merit earned during Saga Dawa has more value than merit earned during the rest of the year.

Above: Buddhist deities are the subject of most *thangka* paintings. Cotton or linen is stretched on a wooden frame and stiffened with glue before the images are painted on. The paints are usually made with natural ingredients, such as lapis lazuli for blue and cinnabar for red. A little gold is sometimes used to burnish the painting. For more formal works, the eyes are painted last during a special ceremony.

Right: Monks at the Kumbum Monastery in Xining undertake with delight the mammoth task of unveiling a huge *thangka* tapestry during the Saga Dawa festival.

Right: Music is an essential ingredient in the making of a Tibetan celebration. Monks are often trained in a variety of instruments, including cymbals, horns and drums.

Centre: Tibet comes alive with fairs as soon as the weather gets a little friendlier. At a summer fair between the towns of Yushu and Maduo in Qinghai, sheep take part in a beauty contest of sorts, a typical occasion for Tibetans to trade and compete.

Far right: Riders flash flags in a rush of colour during the Bon festivities near Aba.

Bottom: Mountains surround a makeshift "temple" of tents under the great Tibetan sky. Few places on earth can be as spiritual. Little wonder, then, why villagers from all over venture into the great outdoors for days on end to pray and commune with their spiritual selves.

Left: Crowds at the horse festival in Yushu watch participants parade in local dress.

Far left (top): During the summer festivals, Tibetans pay homage to the land with outdoor drama performances that involve the use of elaborate masks, costumes and props, reliving some of their most ancient customs.

Far left (bottom): Dawn breaks over a tent site at the height of the summer festival season. Families travel great distances to gather on communal land and venerate the gods on high ridges and mountains.

Above: Tibetans in the countryside in Qinghai perform a local dance at the opening of the horse races.

Right: Tibetan representatives of the local government parade on a float. The message sprawled across the painted grassland on the float promotes government initiatives to help Tibetans by, for example, improving herding techniques.

Far right: White yaks—very rare and very treasured—are displayed at an outdoor festival in Zhongdian. These summer gatherings have a practical bent. Nomads bring yak-milk cheese and butter, dried meat and medicinal herbs to trade with the villagers for agricultural pro-duce, wooden saddles, silverwork and items "imported" from China.

Left: Tibetan children dressed in detailed robes, with large wooden beads in their hair, give a charming performance of a traditional local dance at a temple fair in Tongren.

Far left (top): Farmers in Tongren burn offerings during the harvest festival.

Far left (bottom): Another traditional local dance by fan-waving performers illustrates the uniqueness of Tongren's harvest festival.

Religious celebration takes a different tone in Tongren compared to other Tibetan towns. Instead of *cham* dances and *thangka*-unfolding or prayer ceremonies typically led by Buddhist monks at monasteries, scenes from Tongren's harvest festival seem to reveal remnants of pre-Buddhism Tibetan tradition. Dressed to the hilt, Tibetans in Tongren perform traditional dances that mimic the motions of work in the farm fields. These dances celebrate the growth of the soil and renewal of the land, and the community after the season's harvest.

Left: Riders ready their horses for a race in Litang. Legend has it that the races pleased the gods and ensured good weather for the harvest. Typically, riders lead their horses around a fire in a clockwise circumambulation. When the gods are appeased, the races begin. Prizes for the winners range from wine to simple household products, but more important is the recognition for being the best rider.

Above: Spectators at the horse races in Litang peruse the signage —a picture of the previous year's races. The horse festival, held here in the first week of August, receives visitors from all around the land.

Above (both): The horse-racing festival is not all about the four-legged creatures. Traditional dances and mask parades add more colour to the event.

Right (both): Like many things Tibetan, the rider's dress has symbolic meaning. The bright colours worn by these riders from Kham stand for the elements: blue for air, yellow for earth, green for water and red for fire. The furs often come from tigers or snow leopards, and the riders tuck a ceremonial sword in their belts. It takes about 10 minutes to get all that gear on.

Right (top): Riders drive their steeds to a speeding blur at the races in Zhongdian. Their skill has its roots in the legendary horsemanship of the ancient Tibetans. Horses are revered in Tibet and are associated with strength and transcendence.

Right (bottom): Young monks at a monastery enjoy a mask dance during the year-end Gutor festival. Lamas wearing different masks with the faces of the deities act out the triumph of good over evil.

Opposite: Monks in Litang beat drums to dispel evil spirits at the end of the Tibetan year, before Losar begins to usher in the new year on a high note.

The *cham* dance is integral to most Tibetan festivals. Often performed by heavily costumed performers, mask dances reenact historical events and are usually associated with vanquishing evil and establishing Buddhism in Tibet. Mask dances offer a way to dramatise turbulent psychic forces into energies of wisdom and compassion.

Far left: The struggle between good and evil is a popular topic in *cham* performances. Mask dances often culminate with the expulsion of evil, represented by clay or plaster statues. When the leading deity strikes the "evil" statues with a three-bladed dagger called a *purbha*, it cuts the knots of ignorance and frees positive energy.

Left (top): A dance in Xining depicts deities or gurus peculiar to a particular monastic order. Padmasambhava, one of Buddhism's revered founders, is a favourite character in Tibetan mask dances. His peace-loving traits are portrayed by dancers wearing masks that reflect serenity and mental vitality.

Left (bottom): *Cham* masks are more than just props used to tell a story. These masks, representing the local people at the Saga Dawa festival, show them the diverse potential of their innermost being. The masks help both performer and spectator realise their own condition, paradoxically unmasking their original, free and uninhibited selves.

Masks again, but this is not a *cham* performance. It is the famous opera festival at the Norbulingka in Lhasa. Tibetan opera, or *lhamo*, often serves as a precursor to *cham* performances. These musical refrains are secular in form and often portray the heroics of kings as they battle the evil forces. *Lhamo* was invented by Tagtong Gyelpo in the 14th century. Travelling troupes would often grace the event with performances that might last an entire day.

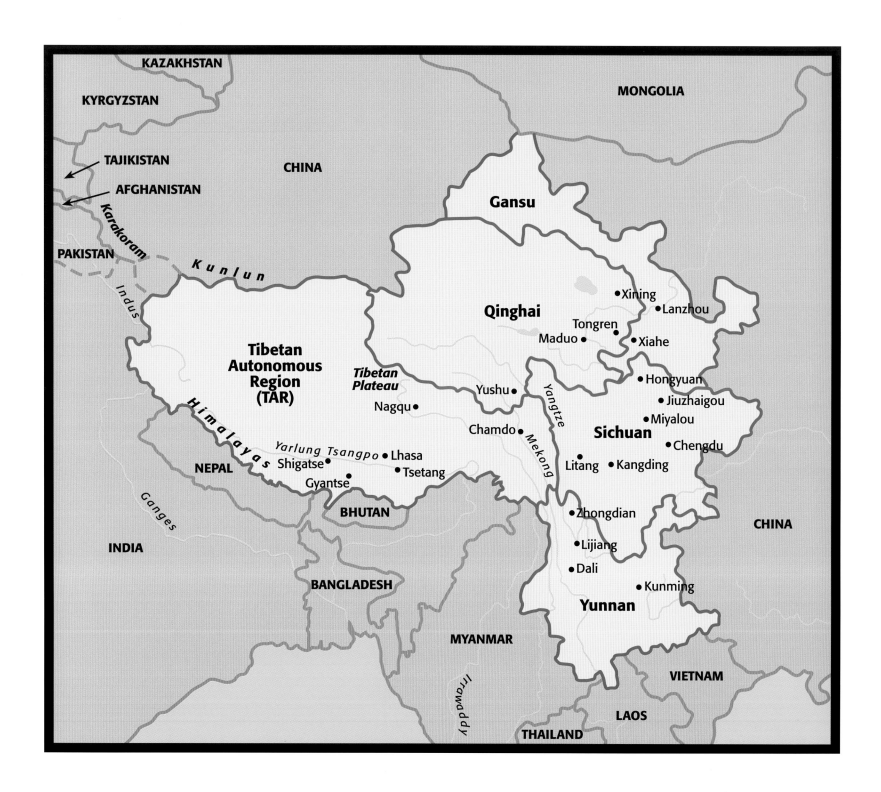

TRAVEL NOTES

By Jimmy Lam

Despite being in the middle of Asia, almost as close to Southeast Asia as to Western Europe, Tibet is one of the most challenging parts of the planet to get to, and to get around in. This final chapter is not intended as a complete, detailed travel guide. What it hopes to do is to give an indication of what you might expect in Tibet so that you will enjoy this blessed land.

Where To Go

Tibet is a big place. You will not get to see all there is to see in one visit. I have been to Tibet many times since my first visit in 1997. Don't stop in the TAR. Tibetan culture is also prevalent in Qinghai, Gansu, Sichuan and Yunnan. The following suggested routes should help you access some of these places and give you a more thorough experience of Tibet.

Tibetan Autonomous Region (TAR)

The centre of tourism in Tibet, Lhasa should take a few days to explore. The roads are good, and accommodation is easily available and generally decent. Go on to Shigatse, then Gyantse and finally Tsetang. The trip takes 10 to 12 days. Another route starts at Chamdo and goes on to Lhasa, then Suoxian, Dingqing and Nagqu in about 10 days. This trip is by far the most difficult listed here. Roads and lodging are nothing to write home about. Be prepared to rough it out. You may also need to get permits to travel through some parts of this remote region. Survive all that, and you will come right up to an array of great landscapes and become well-acquainted with the life of a Tibetan nomad.

Yunnan

Visit Zhongdian, Diqin and the surrounding areas in four to five days, as an extension of a trip to Dali or Lijiang. Driving from Lijiang to Zhongdian takes about five hours, passing unspoiled Tibetan villages and monasteries. This route is sometimes used as a "back door" entry into Lhasa.

Sichuan

The route from Chengdu to Yunnan's Zhongdian provides great insights into eastern Tibetan culture. Plan on spending 12 to 15 days on this trip. Poor infrastructure has thwarted travel in the area, but the situation is improving. From Chengdu, go to Kangding, then Litang, Daocheng and Xiangcheng. You will see unspoiled landscapes, interesting villages with differing architecture, monasteries and, if your timing is right, the horse races in Litang.

Another route from Chengdu goes through Litang, Tagong, Daofu, Ganzi and Dege, before heading back to Chengdu. This trip also takes 12 to 15 days. Roads are not very good north of Tagong, and the places are very remote. But there is a lot of history in this region.

Travelling from Chengdu to Aba and back in mid- to end-October lets you see the fall foliage in all its flaming glory. The trip takes about two weeks. From Chengdu, go to Miyalou, then Siguniangshan, Hongyuan and Jiuzhaigou. Aba will expose you to the different Tibetan Buddhist sects as well as to the ancient Bon religion. There are many unexplored monasteries, unique villages and examples of indigenous architecture. Don't expect much from the roads and living conditions. In winter, there is no water supply, and toilets often do not work because the water freezes in the pipes. But winter is the time to experience the colourful Monlam festival.

Qinghai

From Xining, go to Tongren, then Maduo, Maqin and Yushu. The trip takes about 12 days and lets you see the Amdo region. While Xining is a typical Chinese city, it is also the location of the Kumbum Monastery. During the Saga Dawa festival, the area comes alive in full Tibetan regalia. Tongren has an interesting harvest festival, and you can also get to see *thangka* painting. Beyond Tongren, roads deteriorate, until you reach Yushu, famous for its annual horse-racing festival.

Gansu

On this short trip from Lanzhou to Xiahe, you can visit the Labrang Monastery and breathe in the view of a Tibetan grassland.

When To Go

Winter is a good time to visit. There are few tourists around, and the nomads are usually out and around. But spring, early summer and late autumn are possibly the best times to visit. Plan your trip to coincide with one of the main festivals, such as Losar or Saga Dawa.

Getting There

Chengdu, the capital of Sichuan, has an international airport and is a great place to launch your exploration of the Kham region. From Chengdu, the more adventurous can travel north to Qinghai and Gansu, passing through many Tibetan areas along the way. Lhasa (capital of the TAR), Xining (Qinghai's capital) and Lanzhou (Gansu's capital) have good domestic connections. Zhongdian, in Yunnan, has recently opened up to air traffic. You can fly from there to Kunming, Yunnan's capital.

Getting Around

Travel within Tibet can be expensive. Often, especially in out-of-the-way places, you will need to rent four-wheel-drive vehicles, together with a driver. Consult a travel agency and make all travel arrangements before you take off for Tibet.

Hiring a personal guide is a great idea, especially if you want to explore the nether regions where little Chinese or English is spoken. There are numerous dialect groups in Tibet. Choose a guide who is either from or familiar with the region you are visiting. Tibetans are generally warm and hospitable, and will often invite visitors into their homes for a spot of butter tea.

Altitude Sickness

Much of Tibet is thousands of metres above sea level, so at some point in your journey, you might experience altitude sickness. It might be worth your while to look at a good travel guide to find out the elevation of some of the places you are visiting. If the elevations are considerable, then you might want to take your time to acclimatise before reaching the summit of your visit. You can do this by spending extra days at lower levels before heading up to higher elevations. Some people begin to feel altitude sickness from 3,000 m, so if you expect to go to places higher than that, you might want to take the necessary precautions.

Places To Stay

Let's put it this way: No one goes to Tibet for a resort vacation. Accommodations are, for the most part, a means to an end. Hotels in Tibet have a star rating that is commensurate with the Chinese standard, which is quite different from what you might expect in the Western world.

Accommodations in Tibet hover around the 2–3 star range, meaning that they have attached toilets and hot water. I have slept in monasteries (which are quite accommodating) and inns (once I had to sleep next to the kitchen). In many of these unorthodox places, heating is not a given, so bring a sleeping bag.

What To Eat

Tibet is a geographical paradise, not a gastronomic one. Don't expect haute cuisine there. That said, the Tibetan menu is quite interesting, especially if you have a penchant for the unusual.

Tsampa is a staple. It is dough made from roasted-barley flour and yak butter. Tibetans also eat porridge of *tsampa* mixed with milk powder and sugar. Otherwise, *momo* (dumplings filled with meat or vegetables) and *thugpa* (noodles served with a meat or vegetable soup) are alternatives. For a taste of the nomadic diet, dried yak or lamb can provide sustenance on long drives. Butter tea, or *bo cha*, is served everywhere. For a stronger brew, *chang* (a beer made from barley) is the standard. Chinese food is available in most towns of decent size, and major cities like Lhasa, Xining and Chengdu offer international fare.

You would do well to stock up on snacks and water to last through your time in Tibet, although you can probably get bottled water in most places. To be on the safe side, I usually brush my teeth with bottled water. My advice is to eat only well-cooked food and drink hot water, or else food poisoning might sideswipe your entire trip.

What To Buy

Tibet is a great place to buy ethnic arts and crafts. Just make sure they are not antiques. Law prohibits anyone from taking anything with historical value out of the place. Iconic prayer wheels and prayer flags as well as small *thangka* paintings are popular souvenirs. So are Tibetan daggers, although they might pose a problem with airport authorities whether or not you store them in your check-in luggage. Semi-precious stones are also worth looking at, but a good dose of carpe diem is required. Buying them should be left to those who know their stuff.

Visiting Religious Sites

There aren't too many rules governing visits to religious sites, but common sense and a level of decency is in order. In some of the more popular places, monasteries charge a fee for cameras. (The fees go to the upkeep of the monasteries.) It is advisable to travel with a Tibetan guide when visiting a monastery, especially if you would like to find out more about what goes on within its walls.

Travel Permits

While Tibet is generally open to visitors from afar, there are many areas that require special permits, especially outside the Kham and Amdo regions. These permits can be obtained, through a travel agency, from various authorities, such as the Tibet Tourism Bureau, the Public Security Bureau and the military. Check if your travel agency can secure these for you before you travel.

A Last Word

Tibet provides a wealth of geographical and cultural variety that invariably ignites a burst of adventure in every visitor. Keep an open mind, and travel with an open heart, and you will take from this land a sense of peace that very few places on earth can offer.